The Taste of Dark Blue

Paintings by Tali Neeman Sabo
Words by Vivienne Vermes

Matador
Unit E2 Airfield Business Park,
Harrison Road, Market Harborough,
Leicestershire. LE16 7UL
Tel: 0116 2792299
Email: books@troubador.co.uk
Web: www.troubador.co.uk/matador
Twitter: @matadorbooks

ISBN 978 1803133 287

British Library Cataloguing in Publication Data.
A catalogue record for this book is available from the British Library.

Printed and bound by CPI Group (UK) Ltd, Croydon, CR0 4YY

Matador is an imprint of Troubador Publishing Ltd

To all the wonderful women who gather every summer in Garbicz, Poland, to explore the many ways of being a woman, and to the invisible threads that keep us connected even when circumstances keep us apart.

CONTENTS

Two babies are born

A short time before the Coronavirus pandemic began, I sent friends my newly designed art website. One of the sections in the website was digital collages, comprised of images that I have been creating for several years. I had exhibited some of them in Israel and wanted them to have wider exposure. Each image begins with a photo taken from my childhood album and the emotional memory that goes with it. Then with the art I create around it, it gains a life of its own.

During the first Coronavirus lockdown, the slowed-down pace afforded me plenty of time so I got talking to Vivienne, locked up in her Paris apartment. I adored her lively energy and her way with language. Vivienne had given me one of her poetry books, *Sand Woman*, and I loved her poignant words. I wanted to collaborate with her.

Our exchange gave me a new energy as we worked together enthusiastically. Originally my art was born out of the pain caused by childhood sexual abuse. I was surprised and delighted when, linked to the poems, the images expanded into a much wider scope of meaning. It was as if images and poems were mirrors of each other and our joint creation was born.

On October 12th, 2020, I became a grandmother. My daughter Gal gave birth to a baby girl and so our chain of women expands. I would like to dedicate this book to my granddaughter, Lile. May you grow with love and joy.

Tali Neeman Sabo

Website: www.talineemansabo.com
Email: talneeman@gmail.com

A book born out of lockdown

The Covid pandemic brought with it lockdowns, masks, social distancing and a whole new vocabulary none of us would have imagined: "lateral flow", "PCR" and of course the endless repetition of "You're muted." But muted we weren't. When the first outbreak of Covid hit Europe, I was in Paris, in a flat with no balcony. The lockdown was extreme. No one knew how long "le confinement" would last. Like nearly everyone, I turned to the Internet. Tali, my artist friend in Israel, sent me a link to her website. Her paintings startled me. I felt she was telling my story in pictures. I emailed her with my reactions. She asked me to send her my poems. We decided to produce a book together. *The Taste of Dark Blue* is where our stories meet. It is almost as if it created itself. Every painting found a poem. Every poem found a painting. Its coming into being kept me sane and took my thoughts beyond the four walls of my locked-down world.

Tali and I had met two years before, on the edge of a lake, in the middle of a forest, in Poland. We had sat close to the reeds, in a magical circle of women who gather annually, to exchange whatever gifts they have – dancing, writing, sculpture, art, or just themselves. We come from Poland, South Africa, Wales, Spain, Zimbabwe, Germany, England, France. We share our secrets, our pain and our joys, and let the lake and the land absorb them. The pandemic put us in Zoom boxes on a screen. Locked in, but not locked down.

Lockdown? So random. For some, it meant a garden, walks in nearby nature, a closer bonding with family. For others, the nightmare of being confined with a violent partner. It is with thoughts for the victims of violence and rape that we dedicate this book and any proceeds to the Hasharon Rape Crisis Centre.

Our hearts are with the imagination, which is the stepping stone, the means and the end, to unlocking whatever lockdowns we face in our lives, whether from outside ourselves, or within.

Vivienne Vermes

Website: www.viviennevermes.com
Email: viviennevermes@gmail.com

WHEN THE WORLD STOPS SPINNING

I have the world - so they say -
At my fingertips.

Look, world, and marvel
How I spin you at my pleasure
Here, a healing ocean blue
There, a mountain filled
With a necessary glacier, spikes of rocks,
Here, a desert, sand and hidden gold
Of myths, walked by old, brown feet
Helping in the beat they tread
Toward eternity.

World, I have you at my fingertips
As they say -
Have money, will travel
Will pick a cherry from an orchard or two
Will taste a glass of Chinese beer
If that's too weak, a Brazilian rum,
If that doesn't exist, some rough Dutch gin
Or a tumble in the hay,
Or a tumbler of sin,
Drunk at arm's length
In an Amsterdam bar which is dark
With faces that match the walls

One of those places where no one can see
Who you are, or how
Your world
Spins

Until

The morning after.
World, you move round
To the sun
Like a child, smooth with
Love.
Dawn still.

World, was it only
The fear of you stopping in the night
That kept you at my fingertips

When all my life

I could have held you
In my arms?

The Journey, 2016
Digital Collage

THE GRIEF TREE

Mama, I am your Christmas tree
Look where the baubles
Burst from my girl's breasts
To shine in your living room
Look where my mouth
Stuffed with snow
Almost, almost
Sings you carols
Mama, my branches were
Brought here gently
Hushed by huskies
My white-clothed limbs were brought
To brighten you

Mama, tie my trunk tighter with a golden bow
Don't go below, Mama,
I stop
In the pot

My roots are in the garden, Mama,
There, at the edge,
Where the sea slops up
Its weeds and whispers
My leaves have almost drowned
Nightly since I was born

Tangled with the things
The sea brings in
Bones, bits of people, Mama,
And a bundle so burned
It screams the whole night long
By day it is struck dumb
Dangling with disbelief
Caught in the spear-edged
Leaves, here,
In my grief tree

Mama, tie my trunk tighter with a golden bow
Don't stop, sing a carol, Mama,
Shriek good here till the roof fall in
So the tide
Of my each night's deformity
Will not disturb
Your Christmas cheer.

Cobweb,
2017
Digital Collage

11

CRONE

Nimble, she was, light as a ghost-to-be
Heart a bit dicky, but in the right place
Head very odd, like a puffball
A white end-of-summer dandelion
Falling happily into the wind.
I longed to pick her old bones for their thoughts
To gnaw her old brain for its signs

But she was raucous as a holiday
Wild as the end of the world
So all I got was a black-baked cackle
And a dark-green brew of words
That babbled the song of the mad and the wise, that said:

Stand upside down till your thoughts run red
Tumble down with your ear to the ground, and listen,
For the earth alone drums
With the company of angels

Nurse nothing heavy in your lap,
For love is fragile as a sound
And passion is no plunderer, but a magician's pipe
Smoked in the coupling of breath and laughter

Her eyes were white with snows of no season
My winter's witch peeked out of her cave
To give me a glimpse
Of my own old crone

Dancing,
2017
Digital Collage

SNAIL

This snail demands you see it
This spiral holds secrets
That require time
As a friend takes time
As a flower takes time

You who scurry past
A shadow of yourself
The thin, long grey one
That cannot see the sun
You streak along a tarmac track
Trailing the shroud you never notice
Till it trips you up
Winds you in its white spiral
Whispers in the coil of your ear
Mysteries which, in the rattle of your life
The clatter of your death
You cannot hear.

The snail secretes slowly
This spiral requires time
As a friend takes time
As a flower takes time

As the sun has taken years
To bleach the stone
On which you warm your back,
Leaning, in the morning,
Against heaven,
If you take the time
If you take the time.

Conch, 2020
Digital Collage

MRS. GOD

It's a rough deal, I tell you,
Ours is a noisy household,
Prayers rattling the walls from noon till night,
"Lord, give us this, God, give us that,
Lord, let us win the war,
No, Lord, they won last time, it's our turn."
I mean, you can't please everyone.
I'm sorry for Him, really,
But the power's gone to His head.
I mean, He thinks he made the world in seven days,
Seven days! I was in labour for ten million years,
Chips of rock split my belly,
And came out molten.
Lava exploded from my body,
Turned the universe orange.
I <u>was</u> the volcano
I <u>do</u> consist of layers and layers, and layers.
The world knew it, once,
Statues to me all over the place,
Soil full of swollen-bellied homage,
They were on the right track,
He was the House Husband.
Now I have to clear up after Him.
It's a mess, I tell you,
House stuffed with dogma and ideas –
I don't mind the dust,
It's all those beliefs that get me.
I'll have to have a word with Him,
When He has a minute,
About who really wears the Trousers.

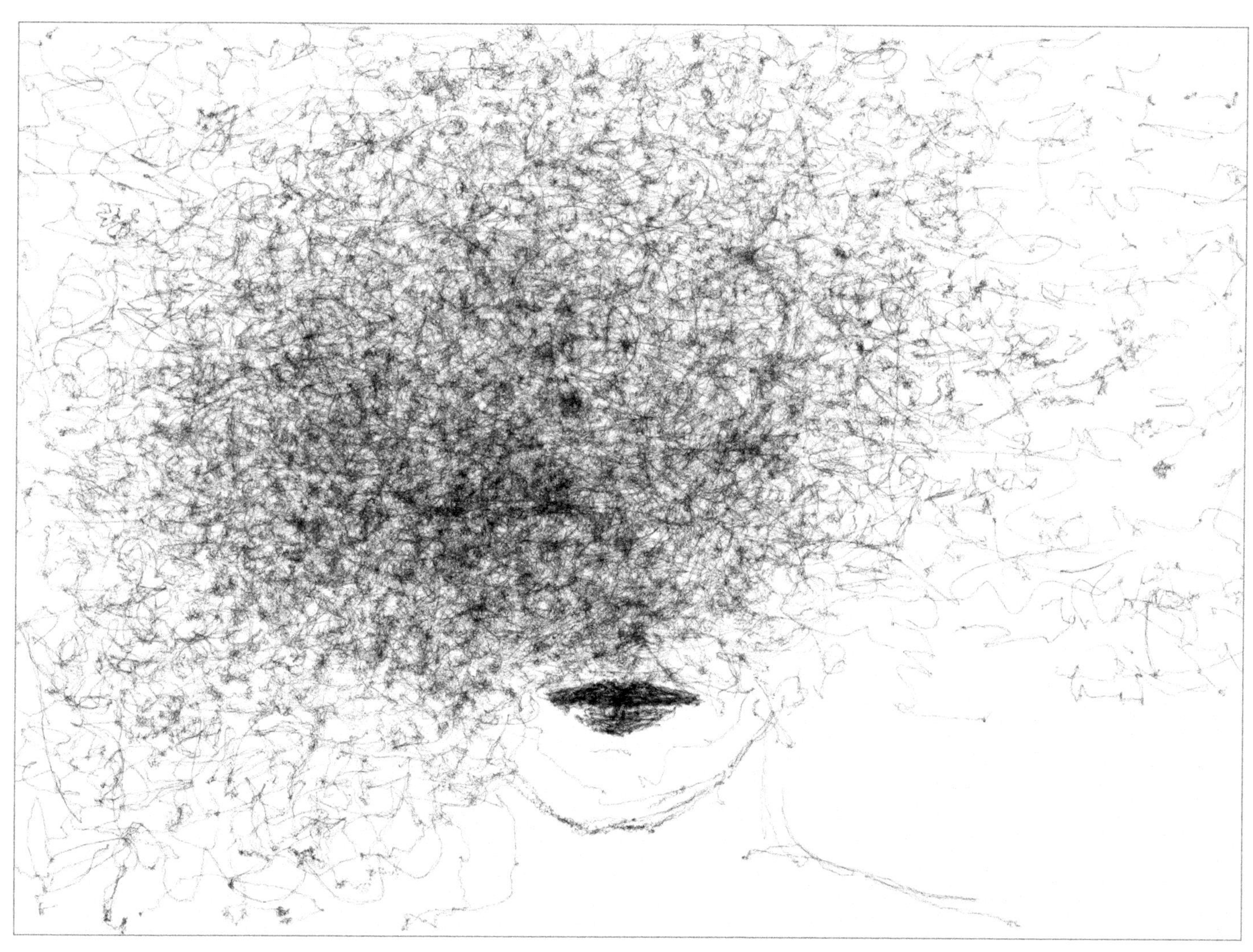

Portrait, 2018
Digital Drawing

PRISTINE CHRISTINE

They called her "Pristine Christine". How they teased her. A pretty child. Never a hair out of place - fair hair, tied into a ponytail with a green elastic band; the cornflower-blue skirt of the summer school uniform always the right length, just above the knee.

"Pristine Christine, always keep yer knickers clean," they would shout, and she would turn her back and walk away in measured steps. Thinking it was true. Each night she put the next day's fresh underwear neatly folded under a white square handkerchief.

She had done it ever since he had left - her ritual, her little ceremony, in some corner of prayer in her mind, her only defence.

"Mummy's little helper". She cleaned and cleaned. Never without rubber gloves. She could go on cleaning forever: every corner of the house, every lingering mark, the fingerprints on the doorknob of her room, any piece of fluff, his skin, his hair that had come too close to her in the dark. She would clean the air of his breath if she could. And if she could, she would clean away time itself, and wipe away the past.

The present took over. She became the golden girl, the one all the boys wanted to date. Long legs, hair shining past her shoulders.

She never married. An only child, she inherited her mother's wealth. Her father had killed himself soon after he'd left.

She bought a house in a good neighbourhood, with manicured lawns and polished cars, two or three to a driveway. She devoted her life to cutting down the trees in her garden. At first she called in the tree surgeons. Later she became a dab hand with a chain saw.

A neighbour, appalled at the massacre, begged her to save the old oak tree. "It's been there a hundred years," she pleaded. "Long before you came, and it'll be here long after you've gone."

The thought kept Christine awake that night. As did the oak tree. It was the branches that haunted her, the way they resembled limbs, thick and massive, looming to envelop her. Tomorrow, tomorrow she would set about the task now that she was well practised in erasure.

A few doors away, into the house, up a staircase and into a bedroom, the neighbour tosses and turns. Does she sleep? Does she dream? The oak tree is there, as it has been all her life. When the house rattled with empty bottles and the shards of spewed words, she would run next door to a friendlier house and hide in the hollow of the roots and look up at the leaves, religious and green, when inside her all was crooked and festering. An anger builds, as she lies in the twilight world between waking and sleep. She wants to kill the woman who would kill the tree.

And then she sleeps.

And in her dreams, roots deep underground are bristling against the soil, and throbbing with a thousand small creatures' busy work in spite of stones, in spite of clogged clumps of clay, in spite of the sudden tug of a greedy beak, still they carry on their never-ending renewal of the earth.

In the morning, she wakes with the familiar pain of the past in one ear, and in the other the new hum of whatever has spoken to her in the night. She decides to go around to the house next door and talk to . . . Christine. That was her name, wasn't it? Yes. . . Christine.

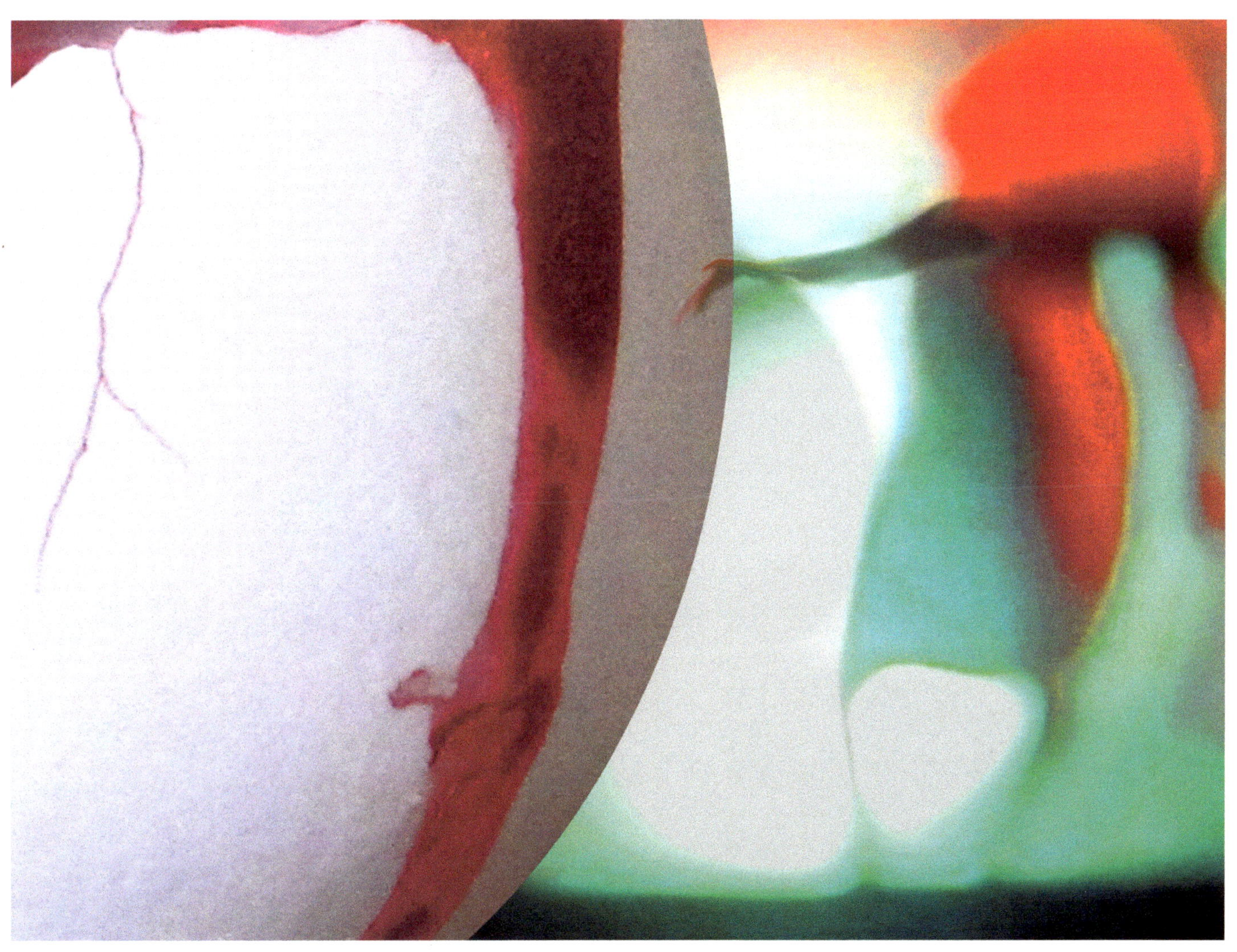

The Heroine, 2018
Found object and Digital Collage

BEHIND THE VEIL

Still witch or wise woman
I swear you were there
Squatting silent at the blood bed
Of my birth
While I was swaddled in white
Bandaged for my beginning
You bundled yourself in black
Behind your opaque veil
Did you laugh at
This business of my
Coming into
Being?

You sat on my child's floor
Black like a crow
You scared me all right
When you lay, stiff,
In my girl's bed
And now, in my mid life
Midnight
What have you to say?
Do you come to harm
Or heal?

Now, at midnight,
Do I dare
To tear away your veil
Black bundle
To draw away your veil?

Behind, beyond, I think,
Is time stretched out in the shade
Is the sun gone mad
And shouting in my hair
Is the dead stone circling
The skies, daring to shine,
Daring to call itself a star,
Is the hand that slapped me
Into being
Is the arm that held me
Angel-like in its crook
Is my first blank breath
Is my time counted,
But luscious,

Is my daring dive,
Is my flying hair,
Is my dead bone I cuddle
Is my teddy bear
Is my adult new-white day
Is my everything
I cannot push into being
Is the muscle resisting
Is the tearing, is the yielding
Is my failure to resist, thank God,
Black bundle, thank you,
Beyond your veil

Is
My birth.

The Protagonist's Journey, 2016
Digital Collage

DESCENT INTO THE MINERAL WORLD

She entered a land of frozen stone. This was a place of great danger. You could get locked in it forever. Perhaps a place of bad magic, with dark figures forever forming and re-forming.

The stone began to shape itself around her. At first it was crystal, transparent. She could see all her loved ones moving, as if on the other side of a window. She called out to them, and it was with some alarm she noticed that they could no longer hear her. But seeing no immediate solution, and enjoying the sight of them, and to some extent the peace and quiet, she did nothing.

It was a while before her limbs lost their movement. It happened while the stone was turning green – at first semi-transparent, like a wine bottle, and then, with sudden speed, it gained an opaque quality, like glass that has remained for years on a beach, washed up by the waves.

Her limbs were trapped in the opaque. They had gone, all the others, the loved ones. She had no idea if they were moving or not, here or elsewhere, in clear air, or, likewise, frozen in opaque glass.

Still, she could hear a voice. She talked to it.

"But I did nothing wrong!" She spoke loudly – she who in life had always been so silent.

"I did nothing wrong!" She felt she was shouting now, and wondered if her speech would shatter the glass.

It didn't.

A deeper voice than hers seemed to hold the glass intact, and her within it.

"You failed to speak out."

She felt the need to argue, although she was unsure what good it could possibly do.

"And is that a crime?"

"There is no crime."

And she knew what it meant to descend into the mineral world.

She in rock, now. She, immobilized. Above, the strata. Layer upon layer, the millions of years taken to create each layer. Somewhere high above, she was sure, rain – vast sheets of grey, beautiful rain – were falling on soil. Trains were leaving stations, loved ones sighing to loved ones.

She lay horizontal.

"To be buried alive. . ." she said.

The voice did not answer.

She knew why she was here.

"It was too painful." Her words were full of soil. She was making excuses now, bargaining.

She had not spoken out. Because she knew no one would listen.

Her throat was closing for lack of air. There would be no redeemer. She alone was her own rescue.

Then it came. The scream. Why had she waited so long? The glass shattered, the earth around her dissolving.

She was free to float up, up into the air.

She was afraid.

She was alive.

She could feel the rain.

Family, 2020
Line Drawing with Digital Collage

EATING PEOPLE IS WRONG
or
PLAT DE RESISTANCE

No and no and no and no and no
And no
You will not eat me for dinner
I may look white
And cream-gentle saucy
But I tell you once inside
My flesh is chewy
Not tender but tough,
And red
All through

You like pale maidens
Well behaved morsels
In anemic stockings
Their bones, if they have any
Will dissolve easily

Hair well-brushed
These maidens have been groomed
They will not moult
Onto the plate

You have me on the menu?
No and no and no and
No.
Eat my hand
And you'll get a mouthful of claws

Beware your appetite

This dish
Bites
Back.

OH GOD, A NOUN

Oh God, a noun.
Oh Lord, words
I love you. You are:
comfortable, naughty, lovable
peaches on my tongue
juicy, easy
you ripen on your own
and pop out
grown up and ready to go.

You nourish
You are heard
You are spoken
You do not require that I
look after you.

Not like the real,
the toes,
the flesh,
the sex,
the house, the walls,
the picture frame on the world
that has hung for too long
in the same place
the hole in the roof
from where we watched for rain

There has been a century of rain.
The clay clogs
You could sink
In the middle of this forest
full of ghosts

They will not go away.

Oh words, I love you

Where the grey world
sucks the body downward,

You fly around the rainclouds
and you play
you play
you play.

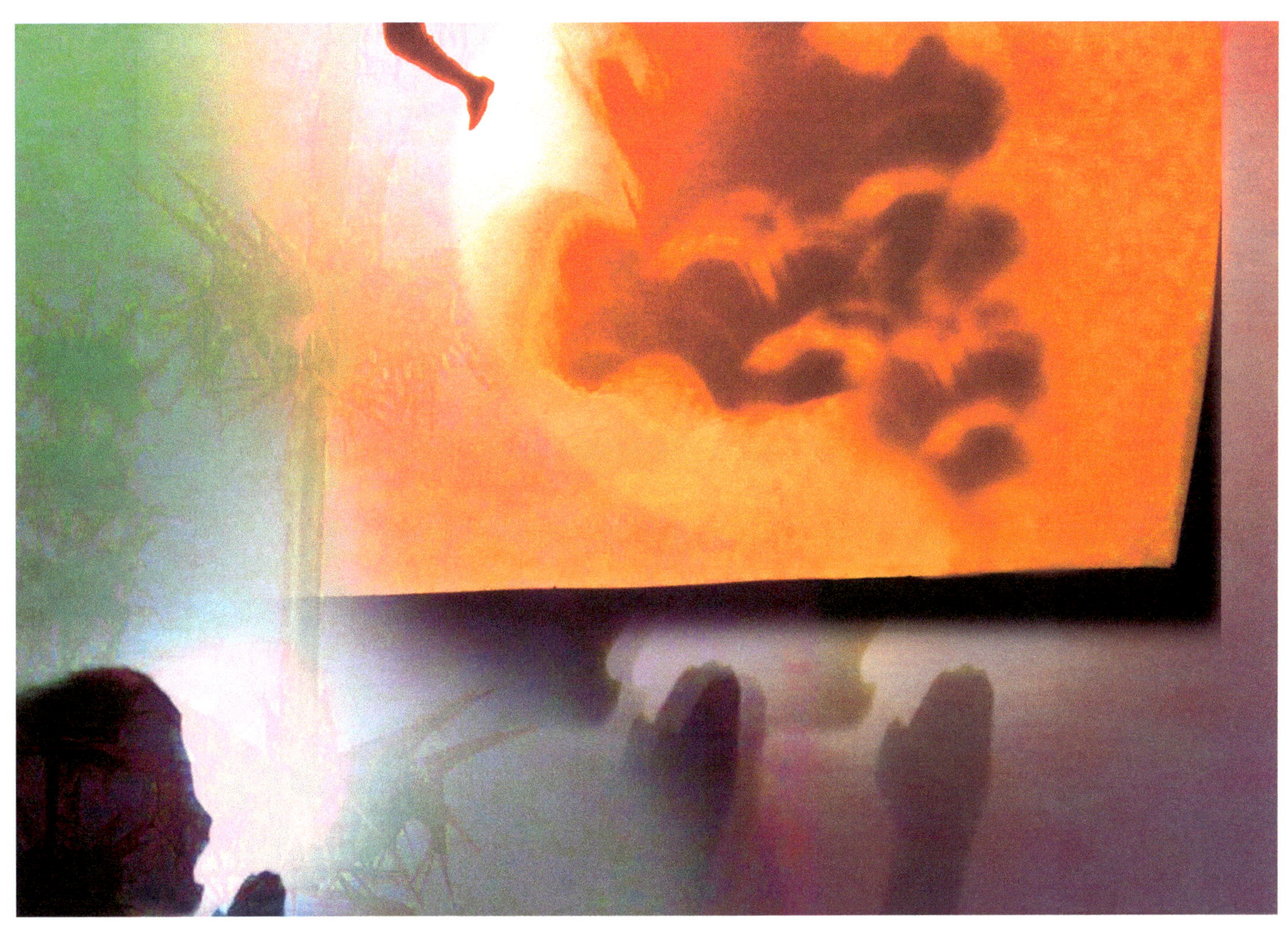

Ghosts, 2016
Digital Collage

RED SHOES

They took away my old red shoes
Said they were dirty
Stained red with currants
Blotched brown with loam
I made them myself
Sewed together in big stitches
Odd patches of soft leather
As irregular as leaves.
Strange, they were, soft to walk in,
The soil spoke slowly through their soles.

When they had gone
I walked barefoot
Through the summer
Till winter came
Colourless.
I ate the skeletons of leaves
Starving, I craved the colour red
As in currants, as in muscles
As in stomach, as in flame.
As in gleaming, as in bright,
They caught my eye
Shiny, new red shoes.

I stole them from a cobbler
Stuffed my feet in,
Oh my, how I danced, with
Fat barons, with
Fast gamblers, with
Brown dervishes, with
Thin gypsies, with
My eyes bloodshot with desire

My tongue dangling like a dog's
Fire in my throat,
No coat on my back, still
I warmed up the winter
Danced my new red shoes
Around the town

Till
They danced me

Till
I was a ghost, till
I was a wraith, till
I was a bone, till
There was little but
My entrails
Dancing.

They danced me to the axeman's hut
The axe on the wall felt my coming
The sweet bright edge cut off my feet
Cut off the shoes
Sweet peace, sweet blood
Sweet axe that stopped the dancing.

On stumps I limp
Through days of searching
For my old red shoes
Strange, they were, soft to walk in,
As irregular as leaves
And the soil spoke slowly
Through their soles.

Red Shoes, 2020

Digital Drawing with Collage

SAND WOMAN

She needs no clothes
Her body wears itself
Naked, terracotta,
Her big beauty dances
From dune to dune
Her foot flow rolls
From heel to toe
Slow, rhythmed
To the space between a morning
And an evening star.

She needs no well.
Her thirst is her own water
Her legs have long since
Opened joyful, wide, wide,
Mated with the wide world
And birthed a flood of beings
Tiny, they trembled under scorpion
stones
Now they crawl upon the sand
Called to her broad back
To lead them in her way.

She needs no way.
Her walking is her path
From dune to dune
From dance to drought.

Follow, but follow.
Bed down at night
Wound and warm
In her desert hair

At daybreak
Don't wait for her to smile
She isn't there
But watch your eyes
Stare, on their first morning
Surprised
By their own
Brilliance.

Sand, 2017
Digital Collage

TWINS

She was born at exactly the same time as me. My twin. My soul sister. My absent other.

"So where is my twin?" I asked my mother. Often. She always answered the same way.

"She's with you. She's right behind you."

I'd turn around. Maybe I would see something out of the corner of my eye. But if it was her, she was gone as quickly as she'd come. Maybe she was never there.

"What colour is her hair?" I'd plague my mother with questions.

"Black."

"What colour are her eyes?"

"Black."

"If we were twins, why do I have fair hair and blue eyes?"

"I don't know. God decides."

I wasn't sure about God.

"How will I know when she's here?"

"She'll be whispering in your ear – when you're afraid, when you're sad."

I was often afraid. Especially at night. I thought there was a tiger under my bed. I had to take a running leap to avoid the reach of its claws.

I told my mother.

She bought me a notepad and a pen.

"Write about the tiger," she said.

I did. I wrote about its glowing yellow eyes, its lethal claws, its fatal fangs.

Then I couldn't stop writing. I wrote about its glossy stripes. I wrote about the ripple of its muscles, the softness of its footpads.

Little by little, night after night, I grew less and less frightened, and more and more interested in the tiger. I realized I was on to something. A tiger? The bogeyman? The witch's house at the end of the unmade road, on the edge of the woods?

I wrote and wrote and wrote.

Later, I wrote about the heartaches, betrayals, loves, losses, the final goodbyes.

I wrote. Or rather, she wrote. I could feel her looking over my shoulder. I felt I could see her. Her watchful black eyes. Her black hair swept back. She was compassionate, yet detached. She could find the right words.

"There," said the ghost of my mother (she had passed into another world by then). "There. That's your twin. I knew you'd see her one day. She's the one who asked me to give you a pen and notepad. She's the one who insisted on filling it. She's always been there. You were born together. You will live together."

"Will we die together?"

"No. She will outlive you. By a long time."

There is so much more I want to ask about my twin. But she is already there, looking over my shoulder, impatient to speak.

I am her voice.

I pick up my pen and write.

Shadow, 2016
Digital Collage

MIND THE GAP

Mind the gap between the train and the platform
Mind the gap between the herd and the hermit
Mind the gap between the blandness of the crowd
And the lustre of your loneliness
Mind the gap between feet on the ground
And those floating in air
Mind the gap between the institution and the
imagination
Mind the gap between the bank and your balance
Mind the gap between fantasy and love
Mind the gap between clever words and cruelty
Mind the gap between the rust of routine
And the electric surge of the blood
Mind the gap between your heartbeats
Mind the gap between words
Mind the gap between the lines on the page
Mind the gap between noise and silence
Mind the gap between who you are
And who you thought you could be
Mind the gap between who you are
And who you once were
Mind the gap between the clinging to the old
And the dread of the new
Mind the gap between the train and the platform

And if you don't, fall in.

This is a place of fear, and flight, and dying,
In the dark, whispers, and unknown hands,
Soft fingers dance, feathers of life
Waltz you to the surface, light,
Another train, another platform,
Mind the gap.

Children, 2020
Digital Drawing with Collage

OUT OF SIGHT OF LAND

The dreams came from the earth. From lying flat on it, changing perspective.

Not from the vertical rush of blood to the brain, but from lying so flat that the flowers looked down on you; from curling into the root of the tree, there with the little creeping things in the spaces in the bark, the whole microcosm rustling, whispering of a different world, calling you to a different path, a winding one, with spirits of blinding colour, where rocks moved as you walked by, where trees waved.

The dreams floated on water.

The stern of a ship, the V of the wake, the greedy seagulls tearing the air for food, wheeling and screeching.

The crew was blind, sailors with drops of water for eyes. They reminded you of lovers, the way they looked beyond you, the way their names kept changing.

Then the fog came, quickly, on a day in midsummer, when all should have been sun. A fog so thick that sight vanished. You groped for the mast, and clung to it. You stayed alive by sound: the rasp of the rigging, the flap of a slack sail.

When the fog lifted, you were thin and brown as the mast, and alone. They had all gone, the sailors, slipped over the side one by one, into the doldrum sea.

You held onto the mast with one hand and staggered around it like a drunken maypole dancer, or a limp shaman, trying to conjure a spirit to guide you.

You looked around, and only when you saw the absence did you kneel down and weep.

You were out of sight of land, where your dreams once lived like dancers.

All that was left was the routeless sky and the waveless sea, and memory.

And the prayer that might blow you back to land.

What Do I See? 2020
Digital Collage

PHOTO

The two trees seem far away,
You can't say for sure they are trees.
Maybe two silver columns, built by
An old emperor, in your honour,
Who loved you, and left.

The street lamps seem far away
On the night of the eclipse
You can't see them.
The darkness is in your head.
A legend. It never was. But –

A beloved figure, in the distance.
It shines, a diamond,
And then goes out.
A diamond? A lighthouse?
Did you see it? Now? What – After?

Don't run to him.
There is no point.
People change when you run to them.
Anyway, no details, please!
No close-up.

If you must,
If you must,
Go closer. To the river.
You find him down by the reeds,
By the swamp,
Far from your white heart's pulses,
He baulks at the boldness of your hands
Trying to catch the silver of his moon.
Futile, the river's ripples have already
Sliced it into pieces.
Your hands are empty, wet,
He does not shine.
Latent. Dark.
Swirling, he covers you.

He has engendered you.
You have engendered him.
Each child and parent
To the other's light, the other's dark.
We will never part.
Here, this is our photo.

Rock Field, 2016
Digital Collage

PANIC

It rises from the sea bed
The nightmare seaweed
Caked in dead fish, dead dreams,
No one warned me it would have
A life of its own,
Fed on all my dead lords,
Bloated lovers,
Hopes over-nurtured
Like spoilt children.
I knew I'd dropped them all down there
Thought the sea would do with them
The natural thing
Thought the sea would swallow slowly
Digest them with its lapping
I did not know grief down there
Grows big on salt and storms
And desperate sea arms
Forming still
This stillborn monster
Wet tree slides into me
Even as I swim.

There are no sailors,
No swimmers,
Nothing solid like a rock
Or the pushing of a birth
Would get this seaweed tree
Away from me.

Not being born, not struggling for breath,
Not that, but this,
The going down, the dying,
The dive to where sounds are buried in the
sand,
To where tears are not measured
For the sea says
It's forever crying.

Here, heaven floats upon its head
And stars swim in complicity
Here, in ancient green light
Where we go has no reason
And terror merely trickles
In and out of all these waves.

Here are no dry throats
Begging for drink and forgiveness,
Only some drowned and gentle sailors,
Only seaweed,
Absolving, swaying,
My hands, calm starfish,
Stroke you, hold you,
My mermaids, my nightmares,
For you are all my dreams.

Drowning,
2017
Digital Collage

METAMORPHOSIS

You leave me a parting gift,
You tie it to my back,
Saying, "Sorry, sorry,
Sorry about the colour
But you always liked black."
I cannot turn around to see it,
But it lives on me,
A dark hump
That grows with the winter
Till I stoop, bent,
A beetle stiff with the weight
Of loss. Not just you,
But every other death that went before
Till I hide in the cracks of pavements
Where insects with folded feet
Shuffle in an underworld
Do their quiet work on this decay.
I belong here
Stunted, without belief
That any other arms than yours
Could lift me to the sun.

In this unmendable season,
A muffled miracle,
The cracking of a shell,
Burst of air,
Uplift into bright green breeze
Under my own
Multi-coloured wings.

I fly over to England.
It has turned brown at the edges
I see you sitting on the lawn
Gift-wrapping a present for her
It is something simple, like. . .
A box of chocolates.

**Freeze,
2020**
*Line Drawing
with Digital
Collage*

SPINSTERS

They call us spinsters. On the shelf.
They see us stiff as old bookends,
Faded as the dull end of the day.

They do not know how we shift with the light,
How we rise with the moon,
Plait stars in our hair.

We are the weird sisters
We spin tales and twirl spindles
Rotate the wheel so fast it hums
The way the morning hums
The way the planets hum

They do not know we turn barefoot
In time to the invisible dancers
Who twist and wheel
Look how our threads tangle and untangle,
Look how we laugh.

We spin sisterhood
We spin poetry and mystery
We spin the silence to listen
To the whispering of souls
We spin around the open fire
That flickers on the foliage,
That lights a track,
We take it, hand in hand.

We stand apart and are part of,
Spinning alone, spinning together
This bright tapestry inlaid with jewels,
See how they gleam
This, then, our magic carpet,
This our craft.

They call us spinsters.

Woven, 2017
Painting with Digital Collage

WHO I AM

I don't know who I am. Perhaps I am
The joke you never finished
The message on the answerphone
The nightlight they lit for you at birth
Because you screamed in the dark.
Perhaps I am the coldness of your skin
Between the sheets
The snow sky beyond your winter garden
I am wherever you are
I think I am your words
Strung together, yellow and white,
A daisy chain.
I am my kiss to you
Your kiss to me
And all the air in between.
And now you say we must not touch
For you have found out
Who I am.

Overwhelmed, 2017
Digital Collage

NOTRE DAME

Our lady, you are wounded
You hide blood in a rose
Men have cut into bits of carved crystal
That most private part of you
Stuck it up on show
Speared it with daylight
Where the cathedral gapes up at the sun
Where the crowd gawps up at your most private crack
Hauled from your cavern
At night, still it seeps blood
Upwards to the womb
Upwards to the heart

It once sat, nudged against the hollow of a rock
It once squatted, near feet flat and loving of the land.
Where blood flowed at the time of the moon
There, later, corn and roses grew
They honoured you, our lady,
Our woman of the rocks
Our maiden of the sea
Our old crone of the sand
Then, fearful of the innocence
Of your young hips moving in
And out of tides
In terror of your hidden fleece
Crouched in the corner of the cave
With screams at the witch's wise white hairs
That dangled from the salt place in between
Your thighs
They launched a cry and speared
That most sacred part of you
It bleeds now, has bled across the land

For a thousand years
Went up in tears and flames
As witches burned in bundles
As women's flesh fell in flakes of dry ash,
Useless, on dry land.

Now you are quiet
A glass rose window
Safe, they think
Red rose in a crystal.

I think not.
I think you not quiet.
I think you a snake
Lovely, curled in colour,
Waiting for the prayer
That will awaken you.
As you uncoil, your curves
Sweep upward, heaving, with the land,
Waiting for the prayer

Our woman of the rocks
Our maiden of the sea
Our old crone of the sand

Our lady,
We pray for you
We pray in the cave
Of your most secret space,
Our lady,

Notre Dame.

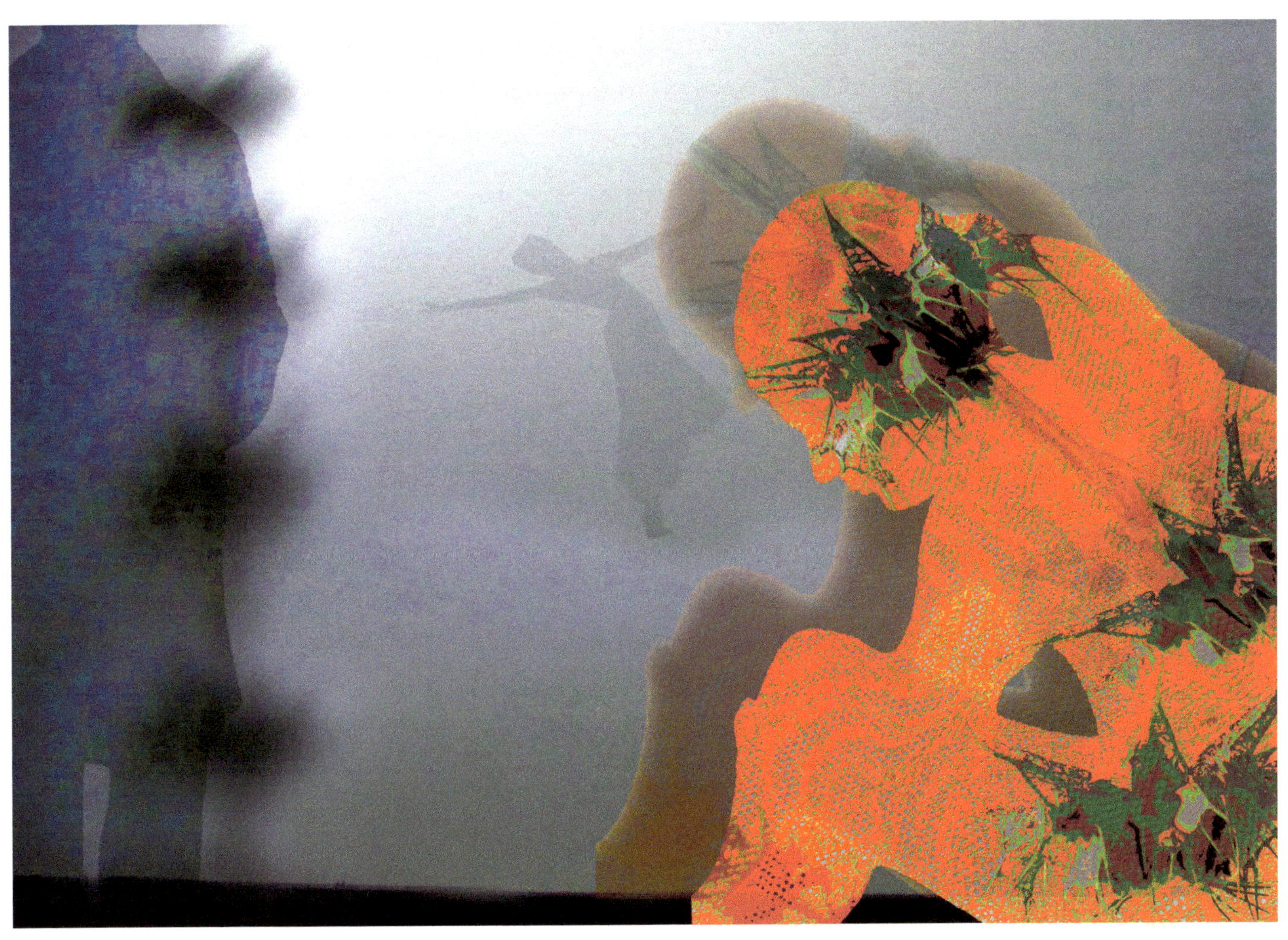

Wounded, 2017
Painting with Digital Collage

THE ROAD

Where has the road gone?
Once, smelling of pine and early flowers
It offered itself to the spread of my feet.
Each muscle soothed by walking,
I met devils and smiled,
Sank down beneath the waterline of green pools,
Fish nibbled at my feet, they tickled.
I rolled in snowdrifts, ice in my hair
Walked along the high ridge, loved the land below,
Walked on my knees, a wild pilgrim with a prayer
Whispered in the spaces where the winds meet.

Where has the road gone?
Shards cut the feet,
Dreams flutter to the ground at dawn
Like wounded birds.
The loved ones who kept our hopes alive
Are now ghosts with invisible hands

They whisper that the road is there,
On the night of the full moon you can glimpse it,
A white ribbon, a shimmer of light,
A mirage, for a moment here, then gone.

Where to? 2017
Digital Collage

THE TASTE OF DARK BLUE

As she lay dying – and she knew she was dying – if she closed her eyes, she saw white. Good, she thought, to go into the white square of ending. This was the way it was supposed to be. Whiteness and nothingness. Nothingness and whiteness.

Her mouth was dry. Now all that mattered was water.

Water. When she tasted it, she had her first sip of colour. This surprised her: water – colourless water?

No. She tasted the dark blue of the deep. In one mouthful, the red of a crushed crab shell, the fluorescent purple of a chameleon fish, the broken rippling orange of the gentle swell at sunset, the smooth grey of the shark's back, the astonishing piercing green of a tiny clutch of algae decorating a rock, making it magnificent.

She did not want to die, then, to go into an absence of colour.

As her breathing failed, thoughts surged like waves: desire – desire for the colour of water, even for a day of it, even for an hour; regret, for the pastels in which she had painted her life, so full of obligations – daughter, wife, mother, sister.

They thought she would die that night. They came to surround her, hold hands, say prayers, cry tears.

"Water," she said, unaware of them, casting them into insignificance for the first time in her life.

"More water."

She did not die that night, nor the next, nor the next. As the days went by, they grew tired of their vigil, and came to see her less and less.

The doctors were astonished. She ate no solids. All she asked for was water.

By the seventh day, her eyes were flecked with amber and silver.

"I want to go to the sea," she said.

They took her to the coast: arranged cars, lifts, drivers - for her dying wish, perhaps?

She sits tonight on a balcony overlooking the sea, on the edge of a continent.

She knows that she can go now, or tomorrow, the way a wave breaks, now or tomorrow.

And there, as the sun goes down on the maybe last night of her life, she raises her glass, and sips again the taste of dark blue.

**No Words,
2020**
Digital Collage

We would like to express our appreciation of the work done by the Hasharon Rape Crisis Centre in Raanana, Israel, where Tali works as a volunteer. The Centre's committed staff work together with many volunteers, offering emotional and legal aid to women and men who have suffered or are still suffering sexual abuse. As our book is about women's journey through life, its joy but also its pain, we would like to donate part of the proceeds of this book to the Hasharon Rape Crisis Centre.